the question everyone is asking

By Bruce Bickel & Stan Jantz

Bob Siemon Designs • Santa Ana, California

Published by: Bob Siemon Designs
                     3501 W. Segerstrom Ave.
                     Santa Ana, CA 92704

Design and illustrations:
Sandy Miranda, Kayo Nakamura, Diane Blough, and Lynn Wu

ISBN: 0-9659733-0-1

CONTENTS

INTRODUCTION

Life was simple when you were young. You were told what to do and how to do it. Years later, life is not so easy.

How do you know how to handle what is going on in your life? How do you know what's *right* in a world that seems to encourage doing the wrong thing?

Many people have discovered a very effective technique to help them respond to the issues and emotions of life. In all situations, they ask themselves:

WWJD?

You are probably wondering what "WWJD?" stands for. It means, "What Would Jesus Do?" Here's how it works: When faced with a dilemma, you can compare your initial reaction to the way Jesus would respond. If there is a similarity – great! If your response differs, then you have a guide for change.

You might wonder whether this "WWJD?" technique can be effective with all of the changes that have taken place during the 2,000 years since Jesus walked the earth. Well, although He lived without the Internet, cars, or indoor plumbing, Jesus was confronted with personal choices like those you face in your life. Modern times may provide nicer clothes and more conveniences, but the issues Jesus encountered are the same as those you face today.

"What Would Jesus Do?" is an important question, but the question alone won't help you much. It is the *answer* to "WWJD?" that will impact your life, the way you think, and how you respond to situations.

The chapters that follow reflect on what Jesus did and said. When you need help responding to life's toughest issues, find out what Jesus would do in your situation.

*Don't become so indoctrinated
by the influence of your culture
that you lose the ability
to think before you respond.
Instead, stop for a moment
and ask yourself this simple question:*

WHAT WOULD JESUS DO?

TEMPTATION

Temptation has been around since Adam and Eve. Everybody has to deal with it. Maybe you're staring at a piece of pie you know you shouldn't eat before dinner, or not at all! Or perhaps you're in a tough situation, and you think that telling a lie will help you get out of it.

In both cases, you're being tempted to do the wrong thing. The temptation may be about something rather trivial, like the pie, or it may be much more serious, like the lie. But until you give into the temptation itself, you haven't done the wrong thing. You still have the option of doing the right thing.

A lot of people don't worry about temptation. They simply do what they want at the time, even if they know it isn't right. If you want to do the right thing, it's important to know how to handle temptation.

WHAT WOULD JESUS DO?

Satan Takes on the Son of God
Luke 4:1-13

One of the most dramatic stories in the Bible concerns the time Jesus and Satan met face-to-face here on earth. Imagine the scene: Satan taking on Jesus, the Son of God.

As he does with us, Satan tempted Jesus when He was most vulnerable. (Jesus had been fasting for 40 days.) What did Jesus do? He quoted the Word of God, which was His and is our final authority. God has given us everything we need to battle the schemes of Satan and the perils of temptation. It's when we try to resist using only our own power that we do the wrong thing and give into temptation.

We need to be totally focused on God and His Word – the Bible. That's what Jesus did when He faced one of the biggest challenges of His life. That's what He wants us to do.

*"You must worship the Lord
your God; serve only Him."*

Luke 4:8

LIFE

Do you ever wonder if there is more to life than what you see around you?

We are all familiar with life in the physical dimension. It begins at birth and ends at death. We try to make the most of the days in between, but is there more to life than that?

Many people are fascinated with the possibility of life in the spiritual realm. A spiritual dimension could give more meaning to our earthly existence, and it could have ramifications for life after death.

What is required to reach the spiritual level of life? Are you required to join a religion? Are there certain rules and regulations which must be followed? How do you make a connection between the physical world and the spiritual realm?

Questions and Answers for a Lifetime
John 3:1-21

A very religious man named Nicodemus, who was sincerely interested in the secrets to a spiritual life, approached Jesus with his questions. Nicodemus had been taught that his religious activities would make him close to God, but he wanted to hear the opinion of Jesus.

Jesus surprised Nicodemus by saying that being "religious" doesn't count – the Kingdom of God can only be reached by being "born again". Nicodemus asked how a person could enter his mother's womb a second time to be reborn. Jesus clarified that the first birth is physical, but the second birth is spiritual. Religious activities are not enough to enter God's spiritual realm. It takes a spiritual rebirth which happens through a belief in and a relationship with Jesus Himself.

Nicodemus was sincerely searching for legitimate answers to questions about spiritual life. He went to Jesus to learn the answers, and he found out that Jesus was the answer. Shouldn't you go to the same source?

"For God so loved the world
that he gave his only Son,
so that everyone who believes in him
will not perish but have eternal life."

John 3:16

PREJUDICE

Do you have prejudices? Your answer may be "no" if you're thinking in the context of cruel racial mistreatment, but prejudice can be much more subtle than that.

Prejudice can be any kind of barrier that keeps you from being friendly toward someone else. Racial distinction is an obvious example, but there are many cultural, economic, and social differences between you and others. Money, philosophy, work ethic, language, clothing, or even musical taste can create walls between people. Whatever the distinction, if it creates a barrier between you and others, then you may be struggling with prejudice.

How can you break through the barriers that separate people? How do you ignore what our culture seems to reinforce?

WHAT WOULD JESUS DO?

Reaching Out to a Social Outcast
John 4:4-26

Jesus rejected the prejudicial social taboos of his culture when He spoke with a Samaritan woman who was getting water from the well. The Jews hated Samaritans, and to make matters worse, this woman had a bad reputation. Any "respectable" Jewish man would have shunned her, but not Jesus.

Jesus was unaffected by racial, social, and cultural barriers. He wanted to share His message about God's love with everyone. That is why He ignored the social differences and began talking with the Samaritan woman. Although she was at the well to get plain water, He was anxious to tell her about the "living water" of God's love.

Let Jesus be an example for you. Stop looking at the differences between you and others. See them through the eyes of Jesus, as people who need to know the love of God.

"But the time is coming and is already here when true worshipers will worship the Father in spirit and in truth. The Father is looking for anyone who will worship him that way."

John 4:23

PASSION

Do you envy people who seem to know what their purpose in life is – those who are goal-oriented and have a clear-cut direction? Do you desire a singular focus in your life like that? Do you find yourself interested in so many things that you keep getting distracted? Are you involved in so many worthwhile endeavors that you can't choose which has the greatest priority?

These questions all relate to your "passion" in life – the one thing, above all else, which brings the most satisfaction, fulfillment, and meaning to your life.

Life without passion isn't living; it's just existing. However, living life with passion isn't easy. You have to find your passion, define it, and then live it. The results are rewarding, but how are they achieved?

Knowing What You're All About
Luke 4:38-44

After healing many people in the village of Capernaum, Jesus was soon surrounded by more sick people requesting help. They asked Him to stay in Capernaum. Jesus declined the offer, saying that He was sent from Heaven for the specific purpose of preaching the message of God's plan for mankind. He chose to be a humble messenger of God rather than a famous physician. It was a decision based on His passion.

Healing the sick was certainly worthwhile, but it was not His greatest passion, His primary intention, nor His motivating goal. He didn't allow other events in His life to distract Him or dilute the importance of His message.

Consider that God has created you, knows your innermost thoughts, and has designed a passion for your life. Ask Him to reveal it to you, and then pursue it.

*"I must preach the Good News
of the Kingdom of God . . .
because that is why I was sent."*

Luke 4:43

CONDUCT

Let's face it. Doing what Jesus would do may make you different. You may end up doing just the opposite of everyone else.

Being different can cause its own problems. What if your friends object? What if they accuse you of being self-righteous? What if they say you think you are too good for them? Should you risk offending them?

To make matters worse, they may call you a "hypocrite" because they know that you used to do what you now refuse to do.

If your conduct pleases Jesus, but offends your friends, should you compromise and try to find an acceptable middle ground?

Get Out of the Shaker
Matthew 5:13-16

Jesus gave two interesting analogies to show his followers the impact of their conduct. He said that his followers should be like "salt" and "light."

Before the invention of the ice cube, people used salt as a preservative, as well as a seasoning. Jesus wants His followers to be like a moral preservative, bringing a virtuous and ethical flavor to their culture.

He also wants the conduct of His followers to shine like light into the darkness, not for their own publicity, but to bring credit to God. Jesus said that a person's "light" should not be hidden. There is no need to apologize for doing whatever pleases God.

Salt doesn't do any good if it stays in the shaker. A candle doesn't do any good under a bowl. Jesus wants you to do the right thing – boldly and aggressively.

"Let your good deeds shine out for all to see, so that everyone will praise your heavenly Father."

Matthew 5:16

INTEGRITY

You know that you shouldn't lie, but there are many circumstances in life when the truth may seem irrelevant. Is absolute honesty required at all times?

What about those insignificant promises that you know you won't keep? What about those socially accepted lies that everybody knows aren't true? I promise to write. It's in the mail. I'll be there on time. It's almost finished. I'll call back as soon as possible. It will be kept confidential.

Are you obligated to limit your promises to those you actually intend to keep? Do you have to restrict your comments to those that are entirely truthful?

Stepping Across the Credibility Gap
Matthew 5:33-37

The truth is sometimes scarce in the newspapers you read, the political speeches you hear, and, perhaps, your own conversations. When Jesus was on earth, society tolerated half-truths, exaggerations, and distortions of the facts as we do now.

The culture in Jesus' time was so accustomed to making false statements that people would often "swear" to be telling the truth. They assumed that taking an oath of honesty would give greater credibility to their statements. Jesus condemned this custom. He taught that integrity and truth only have one level. Extra vows of honesty shouldn't be necessary.

Jesus wants your words to be truthful in every conversation. Honesty, integrity, and truthfulness should be more than just concepts. Jesus wants you to put them into practice.

*"Just say a simple, 'Yes, I will,'
or 'No, I won't.'
Your word is enough."*

Matthew 5:37

CONFLICT

Unless you live alone on a deserted island, you probably interact with a lot of people. Life would be nice if you were on friendly terms with all of them, but unfortunately, life isn't like that. There is probably someone out there whose personality clashes with yours.

Unless resolved, personality clashes can quickly escalate into full-fledged conflict. You and your adversary may both be guilty of spreading vicious gossip, playing "dirty tricks," or just acting in a manner specifically designed to annoy.

How should you handle conflict of this sort? Should you keep the relationship as it is, striking back when you are attacked? Should you confront the problem? Should you surrender for the sake of peace?

Loving Those Who Hate You

Matthew 5:38-48

You have a natural tendency to love those who love you and to hate those who hate you. Everyone feels this way. However, Jesus was speaking to you, along with everyone else, when He said: "Love your enemies."

What Jesus taught goes against our natural reactions. We want to get even – settle the score – stand up for our rights. Anything less may be viewed as a sign of weakness. We don't want to be weak. We think that we deserve the right to retaliate. Jesus, however, calls us to an unusual response. A response in which we show love and forgiveness toward our enemies.

Jesus wants us to change the way we respond to those who oppose us. He asked: "If you are kind only to your friends, how are you different from anyone else?" Imagine how you will confuse and confound your enemy when you respond with kindness. That type of response may change the heart of your enemy; it will certainly change yours.

*"Love your enemies!
Pray for those
who persecute you!"*

Matthew 5:44

PRAYER

You have a lot going on in your life, including problems, needs, and big decisions. God wants to be included in all of it, but that can only happen through prayer.

Praying is not as intimidating as you might expect. It is simply talking to God. No fancy words are required. You can do it at anytime and in any place. You can talk out loud, or you can pray silently in your thoughts. Just remember that God wants you to be yourself and to talk with Him about what is on your mind and in your heart.

What should you do if you want to pray but can't get started? What if you can't think of things to talk about?

Talking to God
Matthew 6:5-18

Jesus could pray better than anyone. It was so natural for Him to talk to His heavenly Father. Jesus wants us to learn to pray in the same way: casually conversing with God.

Many of the prayers of Jesus are written in the Bible. Jesus said that we should not simply repeat His prayers, but we can follow the format. Just as Jesus did, we can start our prayers with thanking God for who He is and the world He created. We can say that we are sorry for the wrong things that we have done. We should ask Him to help us with our problems, the big ones and the small ones. We can pray for other people too, asking that God will help them in difficult circumstances. Our prayers also give us a chance to acknowledge that God deserves our attention and appreciation.

Prayer can be your direct link to God. He is waiting, and He is listening. All you have to do is start talking.

"Our Father in heaven, may your name be honored. May your kingdom come soon. May your will be done here on earth, just as it is in heaven. Give us our food for today, and forgive us our sins, just as we have forgiven those who have sinned against us. And don't let us yield to temptation, but deliver us from the evil one."

Matthew 6:9-13

WORRY

Do you ever feel like you are getting buried by worries? Fretting about your problems and uncertainties can absorb all of your mental energy. Do you become paralyzed by worrying about your situation – unable to do anything because you don't know what to do?

Perhaps you're worrying about family, finances, or friendships. Maybe you are stressed to the breaking point. You may be facing events that you have no influence over. Worrying about an uncertain future can overwhelm everything else in your life.

What should you do when it seems like your worries are consuming you – when the events of your life are controlling you instead of the other way around? What should you do to gain a proper perspective on your life?

WHAT WOULD JESUS DO?

Don't Worry About It
Matthew 6:25-33

Consider the obstacles Jesus faced. Opposition was everywhere. The Jewish leaders were trying to discredit Him and even kill Him. His own followers were dense and sometimes disloyal. Everyone wanted a piece of His time. No one really understood Him.

Nonetheless, Jesus never lost His perspective. He didn't worry about the course of events in His life. He knew that His heavenly Father was in control. He maintained a proper perspective in life by keeping His eyes fixed on God, knowing that everything else would fall into place.

Jesus taught others this important lesson about being free from the burdensome weight of worries. He said that worrying doesn't accomplish anything. He told them to spend their mental energies trusting God to work things out. That same advice applies to you.

*"Can all your worries add
a single moment to your life?
Of course not."*

Matthew 6:27

Priority

PRIORITY

Has anyone ever told you to "arrange your priorities"? What they're really asking you to do is put the goals and events of your life in order of importance. The idea is to work on the most important things in your life before getting to the least important.

For every person, the basic needs of food, shelter, and clothing seem to be the most important – without them you would eventually starve or die of exposure.

However, is there more to life than having your basic needs met? Where should your priorities begin and end, and should they be unique to you? Should you establish short-term priorities, or should you take the more long-term view?

Seek God's Kingdom First

Matthew 6:25-34

Jesus was very specific about the basic human needs of food, shelter, and clothing. He said they weren't that big of a deal! Jesus wasn't being cold-hearted. He was being realistic.

One of the unique things about Jesus is that He deliberately calls people out of the ordinary activities of life to a higher level of living. Jesus cares deeply for us and all of our needs, from our most basic needs for food, shelter, and clothing to those we may not even be aware of such as our need for salvation. He assures us that God knows what we need even before we need it.

Don't worry about your short-term, personal needs. God will provide for them. Make God and His Kingdom – which He is building in this world through the hearts of those who trust in Him – your highest priority.

*"Your heavenly Father already knows
all your needs, and he will give you
all you need from day to day
if you live for him and make the Kingdom
of God your primary concern."*

Matthew 6:32-33

FEAR

One of the first emotions we experience is fear. It's also one of the last. As babies we're afraid of falling. As we approach the end of our lives, we're afraid of dying.

In between, we fear tangible things like getting hurt, robbed, or cheated. We also fear intangible things like rejection, failure, and giving speeches. (Oh yeah, and a lot of us fear creepy things like spiders and snakes.)

Even though fear can sometimes be useful, it can easily become your greatest enemy, holding your life in an awesome grip. Fear can keep you from doing the right thing at the right time. How do you face fear?

Jesus Calms the Storm
Mark 4:35-41

Jesus understood fear. Once He was riding in a boat with His disciples. A violent storm kicked up, so violent that those in the boat feared for their lives.

Jesus, however, was calm. In fact, He was asleep! His disciples woke Him and scolded Him for not caring if they drowned.

The first thing Jesus did was speak to the storm. "Quiet down!" He said. Immediately, the wind calmed and the sea became as smooth as glass. Jesus then told His disciples (who now feared the One who had more power than the storm) that the reason they were afraid was because they lacked faith.

Do you want to overcome your fears? Trust in Jesus. He can calm the storms of your life.

*"Why are you so afraid?
Do you still not have faith in me?"*

Mark 4:40

JUDGING

It is easy to get caught in the trap of judging others: pointing out their faults, and then thinking that you are better than they are. Let's face it. There are people who are worse off than you – lots of them – and finding their faults can be pretty easy (and sometimes even entertaining).

Do you find yourself being critical of others for the purpose, perhaps subconsciously, of making yourself feel more important? Do you exaggerate the faults of others while excusing or ignoring your own?

What is your attitude toward someone else whose behavior falls out of the range that you consider to be acceptable? Are you compassionate and forgiving? Or are you critical and judgmental? How do you respond to them?

Don't Get Caught Throwing Rocks

John 8:1-11

The Jewish leaders brought to Jesus a woman who had been caught in the act of adultery. Jesus knew their motives were evil, so He used the incident to point out their hypocrisy and arrogance. He challenged each of them to examine their own conscience when He said, "Let those who have never sinned throw the first stones!" One by one the men left without further accusations.

This episode shows that Jesus wants us to consider our own behavior and attitudes before we harshly judge others. We should never condone the improper behavior of others, but if we are overly critical of them, then we don't understand the magnitude of our own faults.

Jesus wants you to examine your own life – your actions and your thoughts. If you honestly evaluate your own life in light of what God desires from you, you won't be so quick to throw stones at others.

"Let those who have never sinned throw the first stones!"

John 8:7

PLEASING

God

PLEASING GOD

Have you ever been faced with buying a gift for someone "who has everything"? It's almost an impossible task.

The problem is that we assume the person who has everything would not be interested in anything we might give because it would never be "good enough."

It is also easy to view God in this manner. We think that because He's so mighty and so holy, and because He already has everything, He isn't interested in us or anything we have to give. We conclude that we just aren't "good enough" for a perfect God.

Is it possible to please God? Should we even try?

The Perfect Gift

John 8:12-30

Jesus never doubted for a moment that He was "good enough" to please God. He is the only person who ever lived who could make that incredible claim. How is that possible?

Jesus and God are one and the same. "If you knew me, then you would know my Father, too," Jesus told the religious leaders of His day.

Jesus says the same thing to us today. By knowing Jesus, we can know God. Then and only then will we be able to please God.

Everything Jesus did pleased God. We can't make that claim, but if we think about doing what Jesus would do in every situation, we're going to please God more each day. Jesus is our example. We need to imitate Him if we want to please God.

"For I always do those things that are pleasing to him."

John 8:29

AMBITION

It's natural that you have concerns for yourself. You want a happy family, friendships, financial security, and good health. In other words, you want a great life.

It's natural that you should have such ambitions. After all, society even encourages you to look out for "Number One," to be all that you can be, and to work hard and get ahead.

It's only natural that you would want the best for yourself and that you would do everything necessary to attain that goal. But should you do it just because it comes naturally?

You've Got to Lose It to Win It
Luke 9:23-27

Jesus taught about the great irony of self-ambition. He said you must lose your life in order to keep it. This paradox forces you to choose which is more important: your physical life or your eternal soul.

Jesus taught that gaining everything on earth – all the things that are supposed to make you happy – will still leave you emotionally bankrupt if you don't have a spiritual relationship with Him. If you are willing to give control of your life to Jesus, then you will realize the true meaning and purpose of life. That is when you will really start living – now and eternally.

Jesus wants you to live with ambition and purpose, but He doesn't want your focus to be self-centered and self-directed. Let Jesus be your priority. Let living in His kingdom be your ambition.

*"How do you benefit
if you gain the whole world
but lose or forfeit your own soul
in the process?"*

Luke 9:25

significance

SIGNIFICANCE

No one aspires to be insignificant. Everyone wants their life to count for something, to be meaningful, to make a difference.

Does it take wealth, fame, talent, or brilliance to make a difference in this world? Is it necessary to have power or control in order to accomplish something important? Do you have to be a leader with lots of people hanging on your every word to be significant?

How can you make a difference in the world that will give your life importance and meaning? Can you do something today that will make the world a better place? What can you do that will make your life significant?

Serve Your Way to Greatness
Mark 9:33-37

Some of the disciples of Jesus had been arguing about which of them was the greatest. Jesus surprised them when He said: "Anyone who wants to be the first must take last place and be the servant of everyone else."

Jesus taught that real significance is not a matter of power, fame, or greatness. True significance is found in service to others. Jesus was the most significant person the world has known, yet He acted like a servant. He was always attentive to the needs of other people – being helpful and caring. With a humble spirit, Jesus constantly served others, never demanding that He be served.

Do you want your life to have significance and meaning? Then do what Jesus did by serving others in helpful and practical ways.

"Anyone who wants to be the first must take last place and be the servant of everyone else."

Mark 9:35

kindness

KINDNESS

In a world of selfishness and violence, kindness is in short supply. That's why any act of kindness, no matter how small, is newsworthy.

It takes so little effort to be kind, yet it's not always our first inclination.

Jesus established a standard for kindness when He said, "Do for others as you would like them to do for you." (We call this the Golden Rule.) If you ask, "How would I like to be treated?" in any situation, then treat others in the same way, you will be showing kindness.

How do you make kindness a regular part of your life? Should you do more than memorize the Golden Rule?

Deliberate Acts of Kindness
Luke 10:30-37

Jesus illustrated His view of kindness with a story that is one of the most famous in the Bible. It is known as the story of the Good Samaritan.

In the story, a man gets robbed, beaten, and left for dead. Two important people see him, but they do not stop to help. Being kind to the stranger was just a little too inconvenient for them. Fortunately, a Samaritan man did stop to help. He bandaged the victim's wounds and took him to an inn. He even paid the innkeeper to take care of the injured man until he got better.

This isn't just a heart-warming story. Jesus told it to illustrate the need to be kind in all situations. He wants us to be "Good Samaritans" when it's necessary, not just when it's convenient.

"Now go and do the same."

Luke 10:37

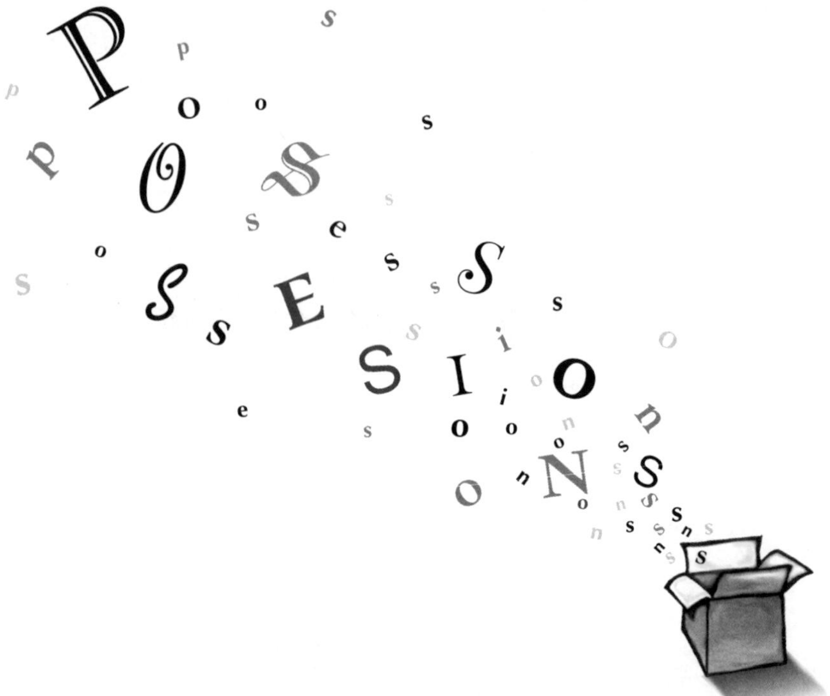
POSSESSIONS

POSSESSIONS

How much is enough? We are told that we need the newest, the best, the biggest, and the most. Society seems to judge us by what and how much we own.

Whether it is name-brand shoes or the model of your car, it is hard to resist the mentality of materialism. After all, we don't want to be too different from our friends. We certainly don't want to be embarrassed by lacking what others have and what they consider to be important. Is there really anything wrong with just wanting to have nice things?

To avoid the quest to possess, should you deprive yourself of every convenience? Should you take a vow of poverty and give every piece of clothing with a designer label to the missionaries?

When Too Much is Not Enough
Luke 12:13-21

Jesus wasn't concerned about owning things. He was born in a borrowed stable. He taught from a borrowed boat. He fed 5,000 people with a borrowed lunch. He was even buried in a borrowed tomb. Although Jesus didn't consider ownership to be wrong, He taught about misplaced reliance on possessions.

Jesus told about a rich man who stockpiled so much grain that he thought he was self-sufficient for the rest of his life. Jesus called this man "foolish" because he only paid attention to his earthly possessions and completely ignored the spiritual dimension of his life.

Don't be like the foolish rich man. Don't depend on your possessions for happiness; they won't last. Find your happiness and self-worth in God who is eternal.

"Beware! Don't be greedy for what you don't have. Real life is not measured by how much we own."

Luke 12:15

SECURITY

What gives you a feeling of security, that sense that you are going to be taken care of no matter what happens? For a small child, mommy and daddy are all that is needed. In adolescence, you rely heavily on the First National Bank of Mom and Dad (knowing that as you grow older the withdrawals become more difficult and less frequent). When you are finally out on your own, reality can be a rude awakening.

Many people look to their own financial resources for their security. They believe they have to take care of themselves, so they devote all of their efforts to earning and saving money. Preparing for calamity or retirement, they are depending solely on their finances for their security.

At some point, however, reliance solely on finances can be misplaced and out of proportion. How should you maintain the proper balance?

Take This Simple Treasure Test
Luke 12:22-34

Jesus taught many lessons about the proper attitudes toward money. In particular, He warned against placing too much dependence on money rather than relying upon God for security.

Jesus gave a simple test to determine whether you are depending on God or on money for your security: "Wherever your treasure is, there your heart and thoughts will also be." In other words, you can easily tell what's important to you by examining what you are thinking about and how you spend your time. If your real "treasure" is your relationship with God the focus of your life will be on Him. On the other hand, if most of your thinking and energies revolve around building and protecting your nest egg, money is your "treasure."

If your treasure is money, you'll be plagued with anxieties about losing it. Put your treasure in the Kingdom of God, which will last forever (and pays great dividends).

"Wherever your treasure is, there your heart and thoughts will also be."

Luke 12:34

DEATH

As much as we'd like to avoid the subject of death, it's hard not to think about it. Death is usually on the front page of the newspaper. Often it's the lead story on the evening news.

Perhaps death is very real to you because someone you love has died recently. You have personally experienced death's awful pain and sorrow. Hope seems to be nowhere in sight.

Is death the final curtain? Or is it possible to "cheat" death? Is all this business about living forever a bunch of nonsense, or is there hope that you will see your loved ones again in a place called heaven? Conventional wisdom would have you believe that there's nothing after death. But Jesus has a different view.

The Final Victory
John 11:1-44

The Old Testament prophet Isaiah wrote that the Messiah would be someone who was "acquainted with grief." How true that prophecy was. From the time His boyhood friend, John, was beheaded by King Herod, to the time Jesus was put to death on the cross, Jesus knew grief and death. Yet He also knew that He would ultimately defeat death, not just for Himself, but for all who believe in Him.

Jesus gave His followers a glimpse of what was coming when He raised his friend, Lazarus, from the dead.

Jesus knew that physical death wasn't the final death. Spiritual death is the only one that counts for eternity, and that's the death Jesus conquered on the day of His resurrection.

"I am the resurrection and the life.
Those who believe in me, even though
they die like everyone else,
will live again."

John 11:25

FAITH

Everybody has faith. Without faith, we'd never leave our homes in the morning, talk to strangers, form friendships, or enter into deep relationships.

At its core, faith is believing that people or things will deliver on their promises, either spoken or implied. Faith is essential to living. The problem with our world is not that we lack faith. The problem is that our faith doesn't go far enough. We are content to put our faith in things and people that will someday fade away, which means that when the objects of our faith die, so does our faith.

For faith to ultimately work and last, it must be placed in that which is beyond ourselves. The question is, how do you do that?

Have Faith in God

Mark 11:20-25

Sometimes the disciples of Jesus were pretty dense. Once they marveled at a fig tree Jesus had cursed the previous day. "Look, Teacher! The fig tree you cursed has withered!" Peter exclaimed, as if he were surprised. You can almost see Jesus roll his eyes and say, "You were expecting something else? Have a little faith!"

In fact, Jesus did tell His disciples to "Have faith in God." In other words, believe that God will make good on His promises. Do you want to believe in something beyond yourself? Then believe that God will do what He says. Trust Him to answer your prayers. Hold on to what He has promised. Nothing and nobody else but God is worthy of your complete trust.

"Have faith in God."

Mark 11:22

LOVE

Loving and being loved do not always go together. Sometimes the one you love doesn't return your love in the same measure you would like. So you try to love better, only to risk being hurt or rejected.

Perhaps you've been on the receiving end of a loving relationship in which you were unwilling or unable to love as much as you were being loved. You probably felt guilty, and you may have hurt someone else in the process.

When it comes to human relationships, keeping love in balance is a constant challenge, but only because we feel the need to keep score. What about God's love? How do you receive His perfect love and then adequately love Him back?

WHAT WOULD JESUS DO?

Love God Completely

Mark 12:28-34

It's impossible to love God as much as He loves us, because by His very nature, God is love. He doesn't have to *try* to love us. He can do nothing else.

On the other hand, our love is fickle. We love when we *feel* like it, and that includes loving God. Yet we are commanded to love God. In fact, loving God is the most important instruction Jesus ever gave.

How do we love God, especially when we don't feel like it? Jesus told us to love God completely: with our *heart* (feelings), our *soul* (spirit), our *mind* (intellect), and our *strength* (action).

Loving God is a lifelong process that involves your entire being. Nothing should be left out.

"*You must love the Lord your God
with all your heart,
all your soul, all your mind,
and all your strength.*"

Mark 12:30

PEACE

Every Sunday, the Santa Barbara, California Town Hall Activists and Veterans For Peace set up 570 (and growing) white crosses to honor our fallen sons and daughters in Iraq. The question we ask is, Can America afford the growing cost of this questionable war in the number of dead and maimed young Americans, the billions of dollars desperately needed at home, and our respect as a nation in the eyes of the world?

www.veteransforpeace.org

PEACE

"Give peace a chance!" John Lennon cried to the world. In a world where nations, tribes, families, and individuals are constantly at war with each other, there is no greater longing in the human heart. We want peace.

Even a single heart can be at war. Jealousy, bitterness, anger, and guilt can make you feel like you are losing hope. Peace, that place of rest and contentment, cannot exist in a restless heart.

Are you looking for peace in a world of war? Do you long for, but cannot find, a quiet, peaceful center in your heart?

It is possible to find peace, but perhaps not in the way you may think. As always, you need to ask the very important question...

The Gift of Peace
John 14:15-31

Jesus clearly understood the difference between "the peace the world gives" and the peace He offers us.

To the world, peace is the absence of war. It is living in harmony with others and enjoying public order. That may be a partial definition of peace, but it doesn't get to the heart of the matter.

True peace means that you are free from conflict of any kind, including what goes on inside you. That's what Jesus meant when He said "peace of mind." We don't need to be troubled or afraid, because not only does the Holy Spirit give us peace, but He also guarantees that Jesus is coming back again.

*"I am leaving you with a gift —
peace of mind and heart.
And the peace I give isn't like
the peace the world gives.
So don't be troubled or afraid."*

John 14:27

INDEPENDENCE

INDEPENDENCE

Why is independence so appealing? Why do little kids tell us, "I'll do it myself"? Why do teenagers seek to be separated from their parents long before they're ready? Why is it so hard for us to ask for help when we need it most?

The drive for independence started in the Garden of Eden, when Adam and Eve believed the lie that they could live apart from God. Since then, we have been constantly struggling to do it our way.

The world is full of self-made people. They occupy the covers of magazines and teach others to do as they have done. It's easy to admire their accomplishments, but is their way the best way? Perhaps we need to look at independence another way.

A Connected Life is a Productive Life
John 15:1-8

One of the reasons Jesus was so controversial when He walked the earth, and why He remains so to this day, was that He was honest. Regardless of whom He was talking to, Jesus spoke His mind, and it was always the truth.

Like a parent who knows his children better than they know themselves, Jesus knows our hearts so well that His recommendations are correct one hundred percent of the time.

Jesus knows that true independence is a joke. There's no way we can function effectively if we are cut off from any outside help. We are like branches in a vineyard. Once cut off, we die. Jesus is the true vine, and unless we are connected to Him, we'll never truly be productive.

"I am the vine; you are the branches.
Those who remain in me,
and I in them,
will produce much fruit."

John 15:5

F·R·I·E·N·D·S·H·I·P

FRIENDSHIP

Friendship. What a concept. Everyone wants to enjoy the loyalty, support, cooperation, and companionship of a friend.

Friendship works like a two-way street. You are there for your friends, and they are there for you. But what if you get stuck with a friend who doesn't play by the rules? What about friends who are always around when they need you, but can't be found when you need them?

Is there a limit to what should be expected of you? How much are you required to give of yourself, and how often? Should you structure your friendships to protect yourself from being taken advantage of? Isn't it reasonable to make sure you have enough left in you to be available to all of your friends?

No Limits

John 15:9-17

When Jesus taught about friendship, He didn't use the analogy of a two-way street (and it wasn't just because traffic patterns were different 2,000 years ago). According to Jesus, friendship isn't a matter of equal "give and take" between friends. Jesus defined true friendship when He said: "Love each other in the same way that I love you." Notice that we are to take this unselfish approach to friendship regardless of how our friends respond to us.

According to Jesus, there are no limits to how much energy we should put into a friendship. He said that the ultimate act of friendship would be to sacrifice your life for a friend. True friendship requires that you be willing to go that far.

Hopefully, you will never be asked to die for a friend. However, there are many other ways in which you can make personal sacrifices for the benefit of your friends through your time, your energy, and your resources.

*"The greatest love
is shown when people
lay down their lives for their friends."*

John 15:13

JOY

Joy is one of the greatest human emotions. They say that unfulfilled hope makes the heart sick, but joy occurs when your longings are fulfilled.

Joy is like a cup that's running over. It's more than full. Joy is abundant. Sometimes joy is unexpected, and other times we eagerly look forward to it, such as when we are reunited with someone we haven't seen for a while.

Wouldn't it be great if we only experienced joy? If life were nothing but a series of happy reunions? Unfortunately, that's not the way it is. Unfulfilled hope and separation are a part of life. Yet there is a way to experience joy even in the middle of your sorrow. Jesus knew all about such a joy, and He gave us a way to find it.

Abundant Joy
John 16:16-28

Think about being in the presence of the most caring, compassionate, and loving person you know. Now multiply that feeling a hundred times, and you may get a sense of what it was like to know Jesus. It must have been a constant joy for His disciples.

Jesus knew that His time on earth would be brief, because He would eventually leave His disciples and return to heaven. That is why He provided a way for them to experience joy just as if He were with them. Jesus told His disciples that they could pray directly to God in His name, and it would be as if He were still with them. They would experience the same "abundant joy."

The same is true for us. We can connect with God and experience His abundant joy simply by praying in the name of Jesus.

*"Ask, using my name,
and you will receive,
and you will have abundant joy."*

John 16:24

BELIEF

There is an important distinction between being *interested* in something and *believing* in it. Mere interest is not accompanied by commitment, but a belief can change the way you live.

You may know many people who are interested in Jesus. After all, He is perhaps the most famous person in history. Jesus only lived to be about 30 years old; as an adult, He never traveled outside His own country; and at the time of His death, He was virtually unknown beyond the region where He lived. Yet even now, almost 2,000 years after His death, the issues of who He was and what He claimed to be remain relevant.

How about you? Are you just interested in Jesus, or do you believe in Him? Do you question whether Jesus is believable? What kind of proof will satisfy you?

WHAT WOULD JESUS DO?

Believing Without Seeing
John 20:24-29

After Jesus rose from the dead, a man named Thomas said he wouldn't believe Jesus was alive unless he saw Jesus in person. Later, when he was personally confronted by Jesus, Thomas believed and acknowledged that Jesus was God.

Jesus can be just as believable to us as He was to Thomas, even though we can't physically see Him. In fact, Jesus expects that we will believe without seeing.

The world has all the information about Jesus that is required. From the Bible and the people who believe in Him, there is sufficient proof for anyone who is sincerely seeking to know Him. Seeing is not required for believing.

Your opinion about Jesus won't change who He is, but it will have eternal significance for you.

"Blessed are those who haven't seen me and believe anyway."

John 20:29

LEADERSHIP

"Lead, follow, or get out of the way." Have you ever heard that phrase? It's rather intimidating, implying that only people who are aggressive and bold can lead, while the rest of us better fall into line or stand aside.

Is that the correct image of leadership? Does an effective leader try to intimidate others and order people around, or is there another way?

Few would disagree that our world desperately needs leaders, but we don't want to be intimidated or told to get out of the way. We're hungry for visionaries who can inspire us to do better and motivate us to achieve more. The question is, where are these leaders going to come from?

WHAT WOULD JESUS DO?

Servant Leadership
Luke 22:24-30

Jesus is the greatest leader ever. Even though He walked the earth nearly 2,000 years ago, Jesus has more followers today than anyone in history.

What is His secret? It is very simple, yet so profound that the most effective leaders both then and now practice the principle every day. It's called servant leadership.

Do you want to be a leader? Whether you realize it or not, you already are. There's at least one other person who looks to you for leadership. Why not do what Jesus would do if He were in your shoes: serve others. It's the greatest leadership principle ever.

*"In this world
the kings and great men
order their people around...
But among you,
those who are the greatest
should take the lowest rank,
and the leader should be
like a servant."*

Luke 22:25-26

REBELLION

In the 1950's, rebellion against traditional society was symbolized by black leather motorcycle jackets. In the '70's, it was protests and peace signs. Now, pierced body parts often express a similar attitude toward society. Rebellion often takes the form of doing the opposite of what is expected or acceptable.

You may not consider yourself to be a lawless rebel, chafing at the shackles of authority, but you might be rebelling in other ways. Maybe your rebellion doesn't take you to the wild side, but in some of the more mundane circumstances of life you may be intentionally doing what you know is wrong. Whether you are at work, at home, or on campus, you may be responding with a rebellious attitude. You may be doing things the way you want, despite whether they are right or wrong. What should you do when you have such an attitude?

WHAT WOULD JESUS DO?

Wanting What God Wants

Matthew 26:39-44

The night before He was crucified, Jesus prayed with deep emotion. He knew the torture that would come with the next day. In His prayer, He asked to avoid the suffering if that would be possible, but He finished by telling God, "I want your will, not mine."

Even when His life was hanging in the balance, Jesus prayed for things to happen according to God's will. His prayer was centered on God's desires, not His own. He expressed His feelings, His emotions, and His desires, but He placed all of His personal preferences within the context of God's ultimate will for His life.

Apply the same approach to the conduct and attitudes in your life. God designed you to be an individual with your own personality and style, but your actions and attitudes need to be within His plan for your life. Whenever you leave God out of the circumstances of your life, you are living in rebellion.

"Yet I want your will,
not mine."

Matthew 26:39

FALSELY ACCUSED

Criticism is tough to take. No one likes to be criticized, but it is a fact of life, and most people deal with it because beneath most criticism is a little truth.

But what do you do when someone accuses you of something he knows you never did? Being falsely accused, especially by people who know you, is difficult to handle. In fact, it may be one of the most difficult personal obstacles you will ever face, and you will face it, if you haven't already.

What do you do when you are falsely accused? Do you proclaim your innocence to anyone who will listen? Do you do everything you can to clear you name? Or is there another way?

Let God Handle It
Mark 14:53-65

Toward the end of His time on earth, Jesus faced accusations that contained no shred of truth. He was brought before the great religious and political leaders of His day and falsely accused of many things. Although they knew He was innocent, people lied about Him because they wanted Him and His teachings out of the way.

Jesus could have defended Himself. He could have contradicted the lies, but amazingly, He said nothing. He was silent. Why?

Jesus was willing to let His life speak for itself. He had lived a holy and blameless life, and He knew that God would vindicate Him. When others seek to discredit you, are you willing to let God defend you? If you are falsely accused and suffer for doing right, don't assume you are the only one who can protect your reputation. Do what Jesus did, and trust that God will take care of the situation. He never fails.

Jesus made no reply.

Mark 14:61

PURPOSE

When we get to the end of our lives, it's unlikely that many of us are going to say, "I wish I had worked harder." Most of us will probably regret that our lives didn't have more purpose.

Having purpose in your life goes beyond getting up in the morning and going to school or work. These activities are important and even necessary, but they probably don't have much to do with eternal significance, which is at the core of purpose. To live life with purpose also means doing that which you were made to do. It sounds simple, but it's a profound thought. It goes to the heart of who made you, and for what purpose you were created.

Do you have a desire to live your life with purpose, to do that which you were made to do? How do you find out what that purpose is? Is there anyone who knows?

WHAT WOULD JESUS DO?

The Ultimate Purpose in Life
Matthew 28:16-20

Nobody knows you better than God – He made you. The Bible says that God loved you even before He made the world. It's a sure thing that He knows what will give your life meaning and purpose.

God made you to be in a relationship with Him. If you're not sure that you're in that relationship, you need to continue reading. If you know God personally, then you are heading in the right direction. All you need to do is read the last words Jesus spoke to His disciples on the following page.

Jesus knows that the one thing that will give our lives ultimate purpose is to tell others about the God who made them. It's the one thing we can do that has eternal significance. Only Jesus can change a life for eternity, and He has called us to deliver that message. He has called us for that purpose.

"Therefore, go and make disciples of all the nations, baptizing them in the name of the Father and the Son and the Holy Spirit."

Matthew 28:19

THE REST OF THE STORY

Now that you have read this book, we hope you know more about Jesus and what He would do than you did before. We also hope you will come to understand something incredibly important.

WWJD? (What Would Jesus Do?) doesn't cut it. Knowing *what* He did isn't enough.

Jesus did much more than live His life to show us a better way. He did something we could never do. Jesus died in order to save us from eternal spiritual death. How does this apply to you? Read these five simple truths and some very important words from the Bible to find out.

1. God loves you and wants to have a relationship with you.

> *"For God so loved the world that he gave his only Son, so that everyone who believes in him will not perish but have eternal life."* -John 3:16

2. You will never satisfy God's perfect standards.

> *For all have sinned; all fall short of God's glorious standard.*   -Romans 3:23

3. Jesus did something you could never do.

> *But God showed his great love for us by sending Christ to die for us while we were still sinners.*
>   -Romans 5:8

4. The only way to God is through Jesus.

> *Jesus told him, "I am the way, the truth, and the life. No one can come to the Father except through me."*   -John 14:6

5. You need to personally receive Jesus Christ into your life.

> *For if you confess with your mouth that Jesus is Lord and believe in your heart that God raised him from the dead, you will be saved.*   -Romans 10:9

Jesus has already done what you cannot do for yourself. He died on a cross as a sacrifice for your sins. All you have to do is receive the gift of eternal life. Do you want to receive what Jesus did for you? Then talk to God with this simple prayer.

Lord Jesus, thank you for what You did for me by dying on the cross for my sins. I want to know You personally and live forever with You. I'm tired of running my own life. Please come into my heart. I ask You to take over. I receive You as the Savior and Lord of my life. Thank you for forgiving me of my sins. From this day forward, make me the kind of person You want me to be. Help me to do what You would do for the rest of my life. I can't wait to spend eternity with You. Thank you, Jesus.

If you just prayed that prayer and received Jesus into your heart, congratulations! Welcome to the family of God! Do you know where Jesus is right now? That's right, in you!

Now that you know God personally, you need to get to know Him better. Here are a few suggestions.

First, get a Bible, preferably a current translation, such as the New Living Translation, which we used in this book, and read it.

Second, start talking to God by praying (you don't need fancy words) and start listening to Him by reading the Bible. If you do this everyday, you'll be amazed at the results.

Third, find a local church where the Bible is taught. Talk to the pastor. Tell him you are a new Christian and that you want to grow in your faith. Be bold – it's important!

You now have the ultimate life advantage. You know God in the real way – He's in your heart. Share His incredible love with others, and in everything you do always ask the question, **"WWJD?"** He will give you the right answer.

WWJD?

WWJD? is a phenomenon that is sweeping the nation. It all started with a group of young people who tied bracelets with the letters WWJD? around their wrists. The bracelets were worn as a reminder to ask the question, What Would Jesus Do?, whenever they were faced with life's toughest issues. It really works! If you would like more information about where you can get WWJD? bracelets and other WWJD? products, visit our website at **www.bobsiemon.com**.

ABOUT THE AUTHORS

Bruce Bickel is an attorney and also serves as a teaching elder in his church. He lives in Fresno, California, with his wife, Cheryl, and children, Lindsey and Matt.

Stan Jantz is a leading innovator in Christian retailing and currently serves as the Director of Marketing for Berean Christian Stores. He lives in Fresno, California, with his wife, Karin, and children, Hillary and Scott.

Bruce and Stan have written four books, including *Bruce & Stan's Guide to God*. Visit their website at www.bruceandstan.com.

The authors welcome your comments. Contact them at:

P.O. Box 25565, Fresno, CA 93729-5565
or
email address: guide@bruceandstan.com

If you have an interesting "**WWJD?**" story about how it worked for you, please let the authors know about it.